# TABLE OF CONTENTS

| S. NO | DESCRIPTION | PAGE NO. |
|---|---|---|
| 1 | BRAND INTRODUCTION | 3 – 15 |
| | Brand Concept | 9 |
| | Brand Management | 12 |
| | | |
| 2 | BRAND NAMES | 16 – 26 |
| | Selection of Brand Names | 21 |
| | Benefits of Strong Brand Name | 25 |
| | | |
| 3 | BRAND VALUE | 27 – 30 |
| | | |
| 4 | BRAND BUILDING | 31 – 45 |
| | Concepts and Strategies of Building Strong Brands | 36 |
| | | |
| 5 | BRAND STRATEGY | 46 – 50 |
| | | |
| 6 | BRAND LOYALTY | 51 – 71 |
| | Tips for Building Brand Loyalty | 56 |
| | Significance of Brand Loyalty | 65 |

| 7 | BRAND POSITIONING | 72 – 93 |
|---|---|---|
| | Process of Brand Positioning | 81 |
| | Elements of Brand Positioning | 83 |
| | Brand Positioning Strategies | 87 |
| | Positioning by Product Attributes and Benefits | 88 |

A brand is a name given to a product or service such that it takes on an identity by itself. Building a recognizable and trusted brand is the goal of every business.

A strong brand is built through the quality of product, quality of service and ability to build trust with the end user. It takes time however and the absolute focus should be ensuring that every touch point a client has with your brand is a positive one. In a small business environment this is more easily controlled, however as a business grows ensuring that the same virtues, principles and processes around quality can sometimes be lost in the quest for growth.

Keeping that focus on quality and service is vital and the time taken to instill this into your staff will pay dividends in the long run hopefully. It's not easy and not every brand makes it.

From our perspective it all starts with a quality product, wrapped up with fantastic service, delivered quickly and easily, has a perceived value by the client, is marketed well and is backed up by strong post-sales support.

"An identifying words, symbols or marks that distinguishes a product or company from its competitors. Usually brands are registered (trade marks) with a regulatory authority and so cannot be used freely by other parties. For many products and companies, branding is an essential part of marketing."

Any brand is a set of perceptions and images that represent a company, product or service. While many people refer to a brand as a logo, tag line or audio jingle, a brand is actually much larger. A brand is the essence or promise of what will be delivered or experienced.

Importantly, brands enable a buyer to easily identify the offerings of a particular company. Brands are generally developed over time through:

- Advertisements containing consistent messaging

- Recommendations from friends, family members or colleagues

- Interactions with a company and its representatives

- Real-life experiences using a product or service (generally considered the most important element of establishing a brand)

Once developed, brands provide an umbrella under which many different products can be offered--providing a company tremendous economic leverage and strategic advantage in generating awareness of their offerings in the marketplace.

A brand is a name, symbol, or other feature that distinguishes a seller's goods or services in the marketplace. More than 500,000 brands are registered globally with pertinent regulatory bodies in different countries. Brands serve their owners by allowing them to cultivate customer recognition of, and loyalty toward, their offerings. Brands also serve the consumer by supplying information about the quality, origin, and value of goods and services. Without brands to guide buying decisions, the free market would become a confusing, faceless crowd of consumables. An established and respected brand can be the most valuable asset a company possesses.

Brands have been used since ancient times. For example, people burned singular designs into the skin of their livestock to prove ownership, while potters and silversmiths marked their wares with initials or other personal tags. But it is only since the second half of the nineteenth century that branding evolved into an advanced marketing tool. The industrial revolution, new communication systems, and improved modes of transporting goods made it both easier and more necessary for companies to advertise brands over larger regions. As manufacturers gained access to national markets, numerous brand names were born that would achieve legendary U.S. and global status. Procter and Gamble, Kraft, Heinz, Coca-Cola, Kodak, and Sears were a few of the initial brands that would become common household names by the mid-1900s. Before long, legal systems were devised to recognize and protect brand names, and branding was extended to services—such as car repair—as well as products. Thus the brand concept moved into the forefront of modern advertising strategy.

# THE BRAND CONCEPT

A brand is backed by an intangible agreement between a consumer and the company selling the products or services under the brand name. A consumer who prefers a particular brand basically agrees to select that brand over others based primarily on the brand's reputation. The consumer may stray from the brand occasionally because of price, accessibility, or other factors, but some degree of allegiance will exist until a different brand gains acceptance by, and then preference with, the buyer. Until that time, however, the consumer will reward the brand owner with dollars, almost assuring future cash flows to the company. The buyer may even pay a higher price for the goods or services because of his commitment, or passive agreement, to buy the brand.

In return for his brand loyalty, the company essentially assures the buyer that the product will confer the benefits associated with, and expected from, the brand. Those numerous benefits may be both explicit and subtle. For example, the buyer of a Mercedes-Benz automobile may expect extremely high quality, durability, and performance. But he will also likely expect to receive emotional benefits related to public perception of his wealth or social status. If Mercedes licenses its nameplate to a manufacturer of cheap economy cars or supplies an automobile that begins deteriorating after only a few years, the buyer will probably feel that the agreement has been breached. The value of the brand, Mercedes-Benz, will be reduced in the mind of that buyer and possibly others who become aware of the breach.

There are two major categories of brands: manufacturer and dealer. Manufacturer brands, such as Ford, are owned by the producer or service provider. The best-known of these brands are held by large corporations that sell multiple products or services affiliated with the brand. Dealer brands, like Die-Hard batteries, are usually owned by a middleman, such as a wholesaler or retailer. These brand names often are applied to the products of smaller manufacturers that make a distribution arrangement with the middleman rather than trying to establish a brand of their own. Manufacturers or service providers may sell their offerings under their own brands, a dealer brand, or as a combination of the two types, which is called a mixed brand. Under the latter arrangement, part of the goods are sold under the manufacturer's brand and part are sold under the dealer brand.

# BRAND MANAGEMENT

## Definition of 'Brand Management

A function of marketing that uses techniques to increase the perceived value of a product line or brand over time. Effective brand management enables the price of products to go up and builds loyal customers through positive brand associations and images or a strong awareness of the brand. Developing a strategic plan to maintain brand equity or gain brand value requires a comprehensive understanding of the brand, its target market and the company's overall vision.

Brand management begins with having a thorough knowledge of the term "brand". It includes developing a promise, making that promise and maintaining it. It means defining the brand, positioning the brand, and delivering the brand. Brand management is nothing but an art of creating and sustaining the brand. Branding makes customers committed to your business. A strong brand differentiates your products from the competitors. It gives a quality image to your business.

Brand management includes managing the tangible and intangible characteristics of brand. In case of product brands, the tangibles include the product itself, price, packaging, etc. While in case of service brands, the tangibles include the customers' experience. The intangibles include emotional connections with the product / service.

Branding is assembling of various marketing mix medium into a whole so as to give you an identity. It is nothing but capturing your customers mind with your brand name. It gives an image of an experienced, huge and reliable business.

It is all about capturing the niche market for your product / service and about creating a confidence in the current and prospective customers' minds that you are the unique solution to their problem.

The aim of branding is to convey brand message vividly, create customer loyalty, persuade the buyer for the product, and establish an emotional connectivity with the customers. Branding forms customer perceptions about the product. It should raise customer expectations about the product. The primary aim of branding is to create differentiation.

Strong brands reduce customers' perceived monetary, social and safety risks in buying goods/services. The customers can better imagine the intangible goods with the help of brand name. Strong brand organizations have a high market share. The brand should be given good support so that it can sustain itself in long run. It is essential to manage all brands and build brand equity over a period of time. Here comes importance and usefulness of brand management. Brand management helps in building a corporate image. A brand manager has to oversee overall brand performance. A successful brand can only be created if the brand management system is competent.

If a brand is not effectively managed then a perception can be created in the mind of your market that you do not necessarily desire. Branding is all about perception. Brand management recognizes that your market's perception may be different from what you desire while it attempts to shape those perceptions and adjust the branding strategy to ensure the market's perceptions are exactly what you intend. So you may now have a better understanding of what a brand is and why awareness about your brand does not necessarily mean you brand enjoys high brand equity in the market place.

## BRAND NAMES

A brand is a "Name, term, design, symbol, or any other feature that identifies one seller's good or service as distinct from those of other sellers. *Branding* began as a way to tell one person's cattle from another by means of a **hot iron stamp**. A modern example of a brand is *Coca Cola* which belongs to the Coca-Cola Company.  The **Coca-Cola** logo is an example of a widely- recognized trademark and global brand.

Brand names are very important for small businesses, as they provide potential customers with information about the product and help them form an immediate impression about the company. A well-chosen brand name can set a small business's product apart from those of competitors and communicate a message regarding the firm's marketing position or corporate personality. When preparing to enter a market with a product or service, an entrepreneur must decide whether to establish a brand and, if so, what name to use.

Experts claim that successful branding is most likely when the product is easy to identify, provides the best value for the price, is widely available, and has strong enough demand to make the branding effort profitable. Branding is also recommended in situations where obtaining favorable display space or locations on store shelves will significantly influence sales of the product. Finally, a successful branding effort requires economies of scale, meaning that costs should decrease and profits should increase as more units of the product are made.

After deciding to establish a brand, a small business faces the task of selecting a brand name. An entrepreneur might decide to consult an advertising agency, design house, or marketing firm that specializes in naming, or to come up with a name on their own. A good brand name should be short and simple; easy to spell, pronounce, and remember; pronounceable in only one way; suggestive of the product's benefits; adaptable to packaging and labeling needs or to any advertising medium; not offensive or negative; not likely to become dated; and legally available for use.

In order to create a brand name for a product without the help of experts, a small business owner should begin by examining names already in use in the market and evaluating their effectiveness. The next step is to identify three to five attributes that make the product special and should help influence buyers to choose it over the competition. It may also be helpful to identify three to five company personality traits—such as friendly, innovative, or economical—that customers might appreciate in relation to the product. Then the small business owner should make a list of all the words and phrases that come to mind for each attribute or personality trait that has been identified. If the brand name is to include the type of product or service being offered, it is important to consider whether the phrases on the list fit well with these terms. The next step is to think about how the phrases on the list would look on a sign or on a product package, including possible visual images and typefaces that could be used to enhance their appearance.

Next, the entrepreneur should narrow down the list with the help of a few friends. It may be helpful to say the possible names aloud, thinking about how they would sound if they were used by a receptionist answering a telephone or by a customer requesting a product from a store. It is also important to consider whether the names will stand the test of time as the business grows, or whether they include an in-joke that may become dated. Once the list has been narrowed down to between ten and fifteen candidates, then the possibilities should be tested for impact on at least thirty strangers, perhaps through a focus group or survey. The opinions of people who may be potential customers should be given the most weight.

Finally, once the top few choices have been identified, the entrepreneur can find out whether they are available for use—or are already being used by another business—by conducting a trademark search. This search can be performed by advertising or marketing firms, or by some attorneys, for a fee. Alternatively, the small business owner can simply send in a formal request for a trademark and wait to see whether it is approved. The request must be sent to the state patent and trademark office, and also to the federal office if the business will be conducting interstate commerce. In order for a trademark to be approved, it must be available and distinctive, and it must depart from a mere description of the product.

**Selection of Brand Name**

How should brand names be chosen? Is the name important?

Marketing theory suggests that there are three main types of brand name:

**1. Family brand names:**

A family brand name is used for all products. By building customer trust and loyalty to the family brand name, all products that use the brand can benefit.

Good examples include brands in the food industry, including Kellogg's, Heinz and Del Monte. Of course, the use of a family brand can also create problems if one of the products gets bad publicity or is a failure in a market. This can damage the reputation of a whole range of brands.

**2. Individual brand names:**

An individual brand name does not identify a brand with a particular company.

For example, take the case of Heinz. Heinz is a leading global food manufacturer with a very strong family brand. However, it also operates many well-known individual brand names. Examples include Farley's (baby food), Linda McCartney Foods (vegetarian meals) and Weight Watcher's Foods (diet/slimming meals and supplements). Why does Heinz use individual brand names when it has such a strong family brand name? There are several reasons why a brand needs a separate identity – unrelated to the family brand name:

• The product may be competing in a new market segment where failure could harm the main family brand name

• The family brand name may be positioned inappropriately for the target market segment. For example the family brand name might be positioned as an up market brand for affluent consumers.

• The brand may have been acquired; in other words it has already established itself as a leading brand in the market segment. The fact that it has been acquired by a company with a strong family brand name does not mean that the acquired brand has to be changed.

## 3. Combination brand names:

A combination brand name brings together a family brand name and an individual brand name. The idea here is to provide some association for the product with a strong family brand name but maintaining some distinctiveness so that customers know what they are getting.

Examples of combination brand names include Microsoft XP and Microsoft Office in personal computing software and Heinz Tomato Ketchup and Heinz Pet Foods.

What are the features of a good brand name?

Brand names should be chosen carefully since the name conveys a lot of information to a customer. The following list contains considerations that should be made before making a final choice of brand name:

A good brand name should have:

- Evoke positive associations
- Be easy to pronounce and remember
- Suggest product benefits
- Be distinctive

- Use numerals when emphasizing technological features
- Not infringe existing registered brand names

**Benefits of Strong Brand Name**

Here are some benefits you will enjoy when you have a strong brand name.

- A strong brand influences the buying decision and shapes the ownership experience.
- Branding creates trust and an emotional attachment to your product or company. This attachment then causes your market to make decisions based, at least in part, upon emotion- not necessarily just for logical or intellectual reasons.
- A strong brand can command a premium price and maximize the number of units that can be sold at that premium
- Branding helps make purchasing decision easier. In this way, branding delivers a very important benefit. In a commodity market

where features and benefits are virtually indistinguishable, a strong brand will help your customers trust you and create a set of expectations about your products without even knowing the specification of product features.

- Branding will help you "fence off" your customers from the competition and protect your market share while building mind share. Once you have mind share, your customer will automatically think of you first when they think of your product category.
- A brand is something that nobody can take away from you. Competitors may be able to copy your products, your patents will someday expire, trade secrets will leak to the competition, your proprietary manufacturing plant will eventually become obsolete, but your brand will live on and continue to be uniquely yours. In fact, a strong brand name may

be your most valuable asset. Brands also help people to connect with one another.

# BRAND VALUE

Brand equity is a **phrase** used in the **marketing** industry to try to describe the value of having a well-known **brand name**, based on the idea that the owner of a well-known brand name can generate more money from products with that brand name than from products with a less well-known name, as consumers believe that a product with a well-known name is better than products with less well-known names. Another word for "brand equity" is "brand value".

Brand Value =    what you get / what you pay   Quality / Price

Some marketing researchers have concluded that brands are one of the most valuable assets a company has, as brand equity is one of the factors which can increase the financial value of a brand to the brand owner, although not the only one. Elements that can be included in the valuation of brand equity include (but not limited to): changing market share, profit margins, consumer recognition of logos and other **visual elements**, **brand language** associations made by consumers, consumers' perceptions of quality and other relevant brand values.

Consumers' knowledge about a brand also governs how manufacturers and advertisers market the brand. Brand equity is created through **strategic investments** in **communication channels** and **market education** and appreciates through **economic growth** in **profit margins**, **market share**, **prestige** value, and critical . Generally, these **strategic investments** appreciate over time to deliver a **return on investment**. This is directly related to **marketing ROI**. Brand equity can also appreciate without strategic direction. A **Stockholm University** study in 2011 documents the case of **Jerusalem**'s **city brand**. The city **organically** developed a brand, which experienced tremendous brand equity **appreciation** over the course of centuries through non-strategic activities. A booming tourism in Jerusalem has been the most **evident indicator** of a strong **ROI**.

Brand equity is strategically crucial, but famously difficult to quantify. Many experts have developed tools to analyze this asset, but there is no universally accepted way to measure it. As one of the serial challenges that marketing professionals and academics find with the concept of brand equity, the disconnection between **quantitative** and qualitative **equity** values is difficult to reconcile. Quantitative brand equity includes numerical values such as **profit margins** and **market share**, but fails to capture qualitative elements such as prestige and associations of interest. Overall, most marketing practitioners take a more qualitative approach to brand equity because of this challenge. In a survey of nearly 200 senior marketing managers, only 26 percent responded that they found the "brand equity" metric very useful.

In simple words, Brand value is that in which People are willing to pay more for a brand than a product. Brand value is the extra money a company can make from its products solely because of its brand name. As an example, how much more is a consumer willing to pay for a coffee at Starbucks as opposed to a coffee at a fast-food restaurant?

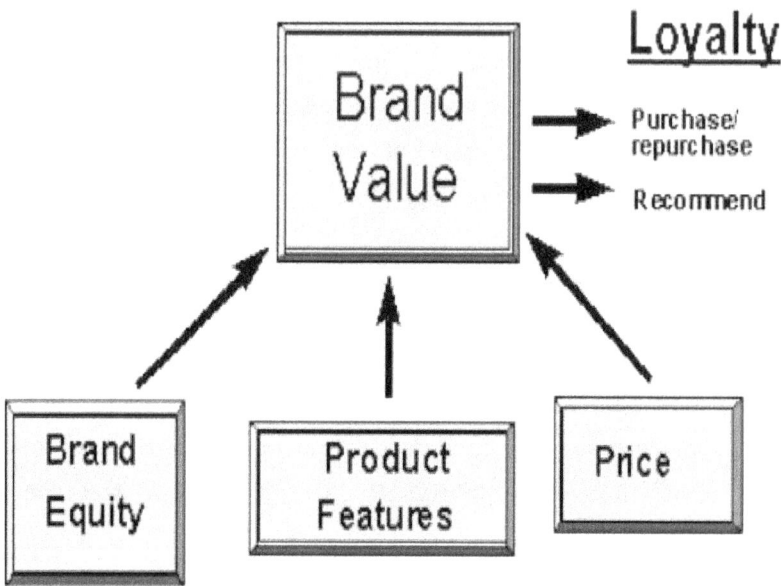

# BRANDS- BUILDING A BRAND

What factors are important in building brand value?

Several factors are crucial in building successful brands, as illustrated in the diagram below:

**Quality**

Quality is a vital ingredient of a good brand. Remember the "core benefits" – the things consumers expect. These must be delivered well, consistently. The branded washing machine that leaks, or the training shoe that often falls apart when wet will never develop brand equity.

Research confirms that, statistically, higher quality brands achieve a higher market share and higher profitability that their inferior competitors.

**Positioning**

Positioning is about the position a brand occupies in a market in the minds of consumers. Strong brands have a clear, often unique position in the target market.

Positioning can be achieved through several means, including brand name, image, service standards, product guarantees, packaging and the way in which it is delivered. In fact, successful positioning usually requires a combination of these things.

**Repositioning**

Repositioning occurs when a brand tries to change its market position to reflect a change in consumer's tastes. This is often required when a brand has become tired, perhaps because its original market has matured or has gone into decline.

The repositioning of the Lucozade brand from a sweet drink for children to a leading sports drink is one example. Another would be the changing styles of entertainers with above-average longevity such as Kylie Minogue and Cliff Richard.

**Communications**

Communications also play a key role in building a successful brand. We suggested that brand positioning is essentially about customer perceptions – with the objective to build a clearly defined position in the minds of the target audience.

All elements of the promotional mix need to be used to develop and sustain customer perceptions. Initially, the challenge is to build awareness, then to develop the brand personality and reinforce the perception.

**First-mover Advantage**

Business strategists often talk about first-mover advantage. In terms of brand development, by "first-mover" they mean that it is possible for the first successful brand in a market to create a clear positioning in the minds of target customers before the competition enters the market. There is plenty of evidence to support this.

Think of some leading consumer product brands like Gillette, Coca Cola and Sell tape that, in many ways, defined the markets they operate in and continue to lead. However, being first into a market does not necessarily guarantee long-term success. Competitors – drawn to the high growth and profit potential demonstrated by the "market-mover" – will enter the market and copy the best elements of the leader's brand (a good example is the way that Body Shop developed the "ethical" personal care market but were soon facing stiff competition from the major high street cosmetics retailers.

## Long-term Perspective

This leads onto another important factor in brand-building: the need to invest in the brand over the long-term. Building customer awareness, communicating the brand's message and creating customer loyalty takes time. This means that management must "invest" in a brand, perhaps at the expense of short-term profitability.

## Internal Marketing

Finally, management should ensure that the brand is marketed "internally" as well as externally. By this we mean that the whole business should understand the brand values and positioning. This is particularly important in service businesses where a critical part of the brand value is the type and quality of service that a customer receives.

Think of the brands that you value in the restaurant, hotel and retail sectors. It is likely that your favorite brands invest heavily in staff training so that the face-to-face contact that you have with the brand helps secure your loyalty.

## Concepts and Strategies of Building Strong Brands

As we have discussed the foundation and basics of branding. Let us discuss through cases how to marketers build strong brands. This cannot be taken up as classroom text. So you need to be very observant now. Wherever you go, whatever you wear or eat have a close watch on brand? Always keep a track of the strategies by companies whenever you go to market to purchase anything. To be a good brand person you need to have open eyes and open mind.

**Steps in Building a strong brand:**

**1. Starts with a quality product**

To build a strong brand you must start with a quality product that delivers superior performance. All strong brands absolutely demand a superior product or service. High quality is a prerequisite to entry so don't think just high quality is enough to set your brand apart from the competition

**2. Identify your brand's singular distinction, define your message and position your brand properly in the market place:**

Once you have a high quality product, then you must decide upon the singular distinction for your product that is most important to your target market. Are you first, best, fastest, or most luxurious in your category? If so, then you may have found your point of singular distinction. You should put a lot of thought into choosing your brand's singular distinction because everything you do will reinforce your singular distinction in your market's mind in some way. An interesting thing to know is that many times the first brand in a category emerges as the category leader can enjoy that leadership position for years and years. If your brand is not first in your category then create a new category so you can position your brand to be first in that category. Being first in your category is often a positioning strategy that allows your brand to be the leader in your category for many years. Federal Express was not the first package delivery company so they invented a new category "Overnight Package Delivery". Not only were they first brand in overnight shipping but they continue to be the leader in the category. Your brand must make people feel better, be faster, do something much better, or deliver a perceived quality of life style much higher than competitive brands. Take the time to understand your category and then position your brand in some manner that makes it very distinctive within the category.

When defining your message, try to own a single word or short phrase in the mind of the market Coca-Cola owns "The Real Thing". Volvo owns "Safe". Nike owns "Just do it". Federal Express owns the word "Overnight". If somebody else in your category already owns the word, choose a different word. The chances are that word is firmly etched in the mind of the target market and they associate it with your competitor's brand. You are not likely to change that impression regardless of how much money, time, and effort you put into trying to take over ownership of that word. The strongest brands that exist today are strong because they stay focused on that one aspect of singular distinction. Once you try to position your brand to be many different things to many different people, then your brand begins to not really mean much of anything to anyone. Positioned properly, your brand will enjoy a leadership position in your market.

## 3. Tap into emotion:

Develop accessible attributes for your brand. Your brand should readily tap into your target market's psyche and evoke an emotional response. A strong brand helps mold and shape that emotional reaction in people, which is a very strong influence in the purchasing decision they make. Once they have an emotional attachment to your product or your company, then they will justify their purchase decision based upon product features and benefits.

## 4. Build the image:

Visually, verbally and through your actions you need to build the message you are trying to create about your company's value. Choose or create a memorable name for your brand. Create a visually effective logo. Write a tag line or slogan for the brand that concisely captures the essence of your unique selling proposition. Your brand should communicate through all marketing channels with one voice, in the same tone, in the same style. In other words, your brand image must remain constant across all channels of communication.

## 5. Market the image:

Projecting the image of your brand should be carried out among all the contact points with your market. This means your name, logo, advertising, and all marketing communications materials should communicate your USP and consistently communicate your brand's message. Don't forget about your website, mailings, sponsorships, and events. Your branding effort must permeate your entire organization. The CEO, the customer service staff, the sales force, the people who ship your product, and the people who sweep the floors at night must all know and demonstrate your brand's singular distinction at every touch point with your market.

6. **Live the message:** You need to deliver on the promise you make to your market. Whatever your brand image, positioning statement, or unique selling proposition, you have made promises to your market that you must deliver on. Remember, your brand is nothing more and nothing less than a promise of value and you must deliver on such promises in the mind of your market. Everyone in your organization must be trained to think from a brand perspective. All employees who have contact with prospects and customers should speak and act in a way that is consistent with your brand's values. Many people call this process internal branding. You'll know your organization is working together to build a strong brand when there is an underlying sense that your employees act based upon what is in the best interest of the brand rather than in their own self-interest or in the interest of their departments. Tell everyone in your organization that the one yardstick for evaluating every decision will be answering the question, "What is best for the brand?". The customer experience must meet or exceed your brand's claims and promises of value. When your entire organization

is clear about your brand's value and promises and everyone in your organization works together to build a strong brand, your market will notice and their image of your company will be consistent with your intended brand image. Your brand can also deliver an enormous sense of satisfaction and enjoyment to your employees-but only if they treat it right.

**7. Measure your brand against the competition and continue to build and refine your brand:** The only way to know how well you are doing in your branding effort is to measure your brand equity against your competition at frequent intervals. This can be accomplished through a variety of market research methods such as conducting market surveys, analyzing the price premium your brand can enjoy, studying the sustainability of your brand, and conducting focus group research. Regular brand audits also will help you assess the health of your brand while uncovering its sources of equity. Brand equity is constantly changing just as society's values and perception are changing. You must understand the equity your brand has in the market and also understand how your brand's image measures up against the identity you are putting forth and the image you are trying to create. When the image you have in the marketplace is not consistent with the image you are trying to create for your brand, then you must refine your branding strategy and project the newly refined identity. Branding is a continuous process of communicating with your market and making and keeping value promises. When you build and manage your brand properly, your brand will be pay you large dividends and your brand will be the most valuable asset you own.

## THE BRAND STRATEGY

In order to benefit from the consumer relationship allowed by branding, a company must painstakingly strive to earn brand loyalty. The company must gain name recognition for its product, get the consumer to actually try its brand, and then convince him that the brand is acceptable. Only after those triumphs can the company hope to secure some degree of preference for its brand. Indeed, name awareness is the most critical factor in achieving success. Companies may spend vast sums of money and effort just to attain recognition of a new brand. To penetrate a market with established brands, moreover, they may resort to giving a branded product away for free just to get people to try it. Even if the product outperforms its competitors, however, consumers may adhere to their traditional buying patterns simply because of their comfort with those competitive products.

An easier way to quickly establish a brand is to be the first company to offer a product or service. But there are also simpler methods of penetrating existing niches, namely product line extension and brand franchise extension. Product line extension entails the use of an established brand name on a new, related product. For example, the Wonder Bread name could be applied to a whole-wheat bread to penetrate that market. Brand franchise extension refers to the application of an old brand to a completely new product line. For example, Coca-Cola could elect to apply its name to a line of candy products. One of the risks of brand and product extensions is that the name will be diluted or damaged by the new product.

Besides offering ways to enter new markets, product line and brand franchise extension are two ways in which a company can capitalize on a brand's "equity," or its intangible value. Three major uses of brand equity include family branding, individual branding, and combination branding. Family branding entails using a brand for an entire product mix. The Kraft brand, for example, is used on a large number of dairy products and other food items. Individual branding occurs when the name is applied to a single product, such as Budweiser beer. Combination branding means that individual brand names are associated with a company name. For example, General Motors markets a variety of brands associated with the GM name.

Brand extension enjoyed a great deal of popularity during the late 1990s. As product development and advertising costs increased, many companies sought to leverage the equity in their existing brands rather than attempting to launch new brands. In fact, a 1998 Ernst and Young study showed that 78 percent of product launches in that year were line extensions. But businesses must be careful not to go too far with line extensions, at the risk of damaging their brand name or diluting its meaning in the eyes of customers. "The corporate landscape is littered with examples of companies that have tried to extend their brand franchise too far," Jane Simms wrote in *Marketing*. "At the same time, other unlikely sounding brand extensions are proving very successful." Just because extending an existing brand involved lower costs, it was no guarantee of success. The Ernst and Young study showed that 47 percent of new brand launches were successful, compared with only 28 percent of line extensions. Simms noted that a brand extension is more likely to be successful when the mother brand is strong, the extension supports and adds value to mother brand, and the extension is valuable to consumers. She recommended that companies considering a launch gauge consumer response by developing new ideas in three ways: as a brand extension; as a new brand; and as a halfway measure, using such language as "from the makers of."

Once a company establishes brand loyalty, it must constantly work to maintain its presence with consistent quality and competitive responses to new market entrants and existing competitors. The science of sustaining and increasing brand loyalty and maximizing brand equity is called "brand management." Large companies often hire brand managers whose sole purpose is to foster and promote an individual brand. In many ways, the job of a brand manager in a large company is similar to that of an entrepreneur who seeks to enter and maintain a presence in a market with a branded product or service.

# BRAND LOYALTY

The extent of the faithfulness of **consumers** to a particular brand, expressed through their **repeat purchases**, irrespective of the **marketing pressure** generated by the **competing brands**.

The **American Marketing Association** defines brand loyalty as:

1. "The situation in which a consumer generally buys the same manufacturer-originated product or service repeatedly over time rather than buying from multiple suppliers within the category" (sales promotion definition).

2. "The degree to which a consumer consistently purchases the same brand within a product class" (consumer behavior definition).

In a survey of nearly 200 senior marketing managers, 69 percent responded that they found the "loyalty" metric very useful.

## Definition of 'Brand Loyalty'

When consumers become committed to your brand and make repeat purchases over time. Brand loyalty is a result of consumer behavior and is affected by a person's preferences. Loyal customers will consistently purchase products from their preferred brands, regardless of convenience or price. Companies will often use different marketing strategies to cultivate loyal customers, be it is through loyalty programs (i.e. rewards programs) or trials and incentives (ex. samples and free gifts).

**Purpose**

Brand loyalty, in marketing, consists of a **consumer**'s commitment to repurchase or otherwise continue using the **brand** and can be demonstrated by repeated buying of a product or service, or other positive behaviors such as word of mouth advocacy.[3]

**Examples of brand loyalty promotions**

- My Coke Rewards
- Pepsi Stuff
- Marriott Rewards

## Construction

Brand loyalty is more than simple repurchasing, however. Customers may repurchase a brand due to situational constraints (such as **vendor lock-in**), a lack of viable alternatives, or out of convenience.[4] Such loyalty is referred to as "spurious loyalty". True brand loyalty exists when customers have a high relative attitude toward the brand which is then exhibited through repurchase behavior.[3] This type of loyalty can be a great asset to the firm: customers are willing to pay higher prices, they may cost less to serve, and can bring new customers to the firm. For example, if Joe has brand loyalty to Company A he will purchase Company A's products even if Company B's are cheaper and/or of a higher quality.

From the point of view of many marketers, loyalty to the brand — in terms of consumer usage — is a key factor.

## Usage rate

Most important of all, in this context, is usually the 'rate' of usage, to which the **Pareto 80-20 Rule** applies. Kotler's heavy users' are likely to be disproportionately important to the brand (typically, 20 percent of users accounting for 80 percent of usage — and of suppliers' profit). As a result, suppliers often segment their customers into 'heavy', 'medium' and 'light' users; as far as they can, they target 'heavy users'.

**Loyalty**

A second dimension, however, is whether the customer is committed to the brand. Philip Kotler, again, defines four patterns of behavior:

1. Hard-core Loyal - who buy the brand all the time?
2. Split Loyal - loyal to two or three brands.
3. Shifting Loyal - moving from one brand to another.
4. Switchers - with no loyalty (possibly 'deal-prone', constantly looking for **bargains** or '**vanity** prone', looking for something different).

**Factors influencing brand loyalty**

It has been suggested that loyalty includes some degree of pre-dispositional commitment toward a brand. Brand loyalty is viewed as multidimensional construct. It is determined by several distinct psychological processes and it entails multivariate measurements. Customers' perceived **value**, brand trust, customers' **satisfaction**, repeat purchase behavior, and commitment are found to be the key influencing factors of brand loyalty. Commitment and repeated purchase behavior are considered as necessary conditions for brand loyalty followed by perceived value, satisfaction, and brand trust. **Fred Reichheld**, One of the most influential writers on brand loyalty, claimed that enhancing customer loyalty could have dramatic effects on **profitability**. Among the benefits from brand loyalty — specifically, longer tenure or staying as a customer for longer — was said to be lower sensitivity to price. This claim had not been empirically tested until recently. Recent research found evidence that longer-term customers were indeed less sensitive to price increases.

**Industrial markets**

In **industrial markets**, organizations regard the 'heavy users' as 'major accounts' to be handled by senior sales personnel and even managers; whereas the 'light users' may be handled by the general sales force or by a dealer.

## Portfolios of brands

**Andrew Ehrenberg**, then of the **London Business School** said that consumers buy 'portfolios of brands'. They switch regularly between brands, often because they simply want a change. Thus, 'brand penetration' or 'brand share' reflects only a statistical chance that the majority of customers will buy that brand next time as part of a portfolio of brands they favor. It does not guarantee that they will stay loyal.

Influencing the statistical probabilities facing a consumer choosing from a **portfolio** of preferred brands, which is required in this context, is a very different role for a brand manager; compared with the — much simpler — one traditionally described of recruiting and holding dedicated customers. The concept also emphasizes the need for managing continuity.

## Six Tips for Building Brand Loyalty:

According to Jordan Media, "87% of businesses do not ask their customers for more business, yet your customers are 3 times more likely to do business with you." That means existing customers are more profitable than new ones. That means you need to build brand loyalty among these customers.

The good news is you can build brand loyalty for your company or your personal brand. Here
Are six things to consider when building brand loyalty:

## Brand loyalty is not just about keeping in touch

The mortgage broker who helped my husband and me purchase our house kept us on his email and direct mailing lists for 2 years after the closing. He constantly sent us information about purchasing a home (which we had already done, and weren't planning to do again for at least five years) and refinancing (at higher interest rates than we currently had). One day, I finally emailed him and asked to be removed from the lists.

Naturally, he asked if he had done something wrong. He hadn't done anything wrong when we worked with him on our first home loan; but the information he was sending wasn't useful to us, so I opted out.

You see, my mortgage broker wasn't thinking about anything more than keeping in touch with the customer so that the next time we needed a home loan, he could help us. Keeping in touch doesn't build brand loyalty on its own though. Instead, he should have thought about what we, as new home owners, needed. If his newsletter had been about home decorating, or resolving disputes with neighbours, or changes in home insurance policies for my area, I would have gladly stayed on the list.

**Social media lets customers connect with brands on their terms**

**Sometimes social media is the best, most unobtrusive way to stay connected to customers, as opposed to constantly emailing or direct mailing them, because they can opt-in.** Sure, social media how lower response rates than email, but it's a better vehicle for building relationships that could be more profitable in the long run.

We live in a world of happenstance, where we can't constantly be monitoring everything relevant to us at all times. Social media is a better way to connect with customers because it keeps the brand at the top of their minds without bombarding them with so much information they opt out. Your fans may not purchase today, tomorrow, or even three months from now; but when they need the product or service you are offering, they will remember that you give lots of coupons, or have lots of people who like your updates, or share lots of useful and relevant information. They will come to you first.

## Brand Loyalty depends on high switching costs

**Creating higher switching costs is an easy way to keep customers from going to a competitor, but make sure you do it right!** The most notorious industry for high switching costs is the cell phone industry, with exorbitant contract cancellation fees.

I am not advocating that you take the same stance as the cell phone industry by any means. But I do think you can create high switching costs no matter what your product or service is.

For example, take **Dan Schawbel**. He is simply THE authority in **personal branding**. We're friends, but even if we weren't, I couldn't stop following him on Twitter and

Google Reader if I tried. He shares the best, most comprehensive content about personal branding today. Even if I only read a fraction of what he puts out, I'm fairly up-to-date on what I need to be doing to manage my career in the social age.

That's a switching cost. It costs me energy to switch to another source for personal branding advice. How can you introduce switching costs to your personal brand?

**Brand loyalty means rewarding your customers.**

**One easy way to create brand loyalty is a customer reward program.** The program doesn't have to be anything fancy. Here are some ideas:

- sharing coupons with fans and followers on certain social media accounts
- emailing special promotion codes to customers who purchase a certain amount

- hosting giveaways specifically for repeat customers
- celebrating a holiday like Alice is doing with Earth Day
- providing a special free report in your subscriber footer

These programs also don't have to be expensive. You can offer products and services you already have as incentives, as many companies do. And why not? True fans want more of what you already have.

**Talkative brand loyalists are the most valuable asset any company can have**

**In the book,** THE INFLUENTIAL, **the authors explain why one American in ten tells the other nine how to vote, where to eat, and what to buy.** Wouldn't you like to get your products and services into the hands of these people?

Well, chances are, a percentage of your customers are already influencers in your category; you just need to find them and activate them. Your most loyal customers are your fan base, and often are the best people to share their experiences with your company. It's not enough just to have influencers; you also need to give them a conversation starter and a place to have that conversation. For example, many companies offer brand loyalty incentives, such as a gift card when you refer a friend. By giving your loyal customers reasons to talk about you, you can create buzz and gain new customers.

**Brand loyalty is not just about discounts; it's about training your fan base to visit regularly**

**When companies continuously give coupons to their loyal customers, it effectively lowers the price of the product.** One retail chain in St. Louis put coupons for 15% off in the weekend paper, every single weekend. Their customers became accustomed to discounts, and stopped purchasing anything at full price!

Brand loyalty is not just about coupons, promotions, and discounts. It's not just about giving everything away for free on your blog. Those are merely vehicles to get your fan base talking or give your fan base a reason to stop back. If you plan to use discounts to create brand loyalty, make sure your promotions are irregular and unpredictable. This even gives customers more incentive to follow you on social media outlets.

## Significance of Brand loyalty

Brand loyalty determines that to what extent the consumer is loyal to the brand. Its basically the attitude which is reflected in one's behavior. The feelings consumer have towards the brand results in changing the buying behavior pattern of the consumers that can be determined when the buyer prefers the one brand over the other and consumes it. The number of times the brand is purchase and consumed by the buyer and repeated sales of the brand all are the reflections of brand loyalty. Brand is considered to be the credible source of providing the quality. So it is clearly mentioned in the definition the brand that how important the quality matters in building the brand and in establishing the positive attitudes towards the brand in the form of brand loyalty.

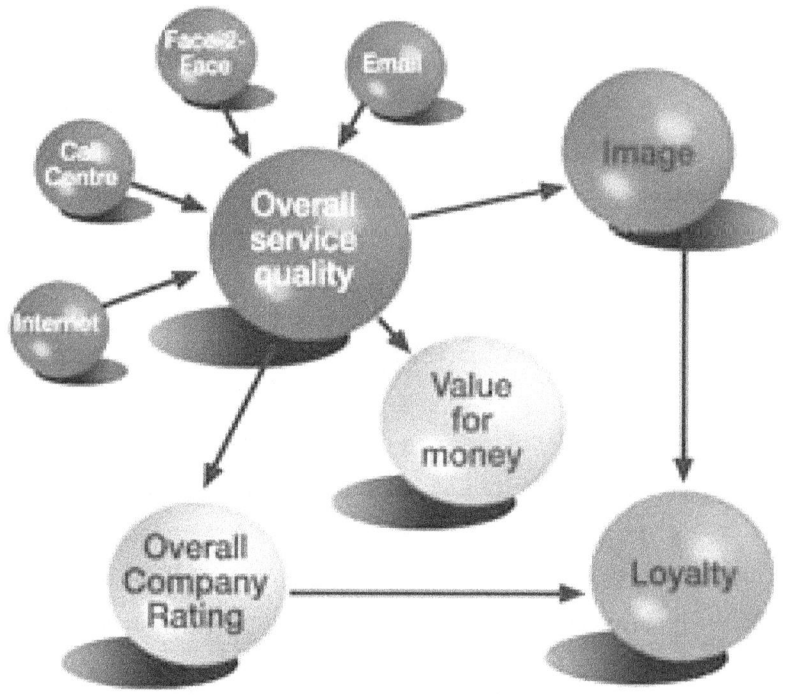

As the number of brands increase in the market, the competition gets intensified with that the options for the buyers also becomes available and the degree of brand loyalty also decreases with it. So In order to tie the consumers to the brand .it is important for the marketer to maintain and improve the quality with consistency. Perceived risk is an important factor which incessantly has its influence on brand loyalty. The people with more perceived risk tend to be more loyal than those of the consumers having low perceived risk, because the people with higher perceived risk do not really want to change their brand on the regular basis, due to the risk involved in trying the new brand.

Brand loyalty the gem of all gems. Repeat customers who without thinking twice or even considering other options are the cream of the crop. Every business aspires to be the "go to" and have that loyalty. Loyalty is built based upon relationships and a sense of belonging. Relationships are built from trust which are stemmed from conversation, exceptional customer service, a website or store that has the product/service desired easily accessible with a trustworthy check out. The conversation cannot be built without awareness and a willingness to buy OR be a part of. I stress the BEING A PART OF as there is an emotional connection of BEING A PART OF, interacting with the overall experience. Brand loyalty comes in different forms and is spread across various industries. Sports teams, we associate with a team that we like and become a part of a group. We support that team and bleed their colors. Why? We do not know them but yet we watch them religiously, wear their jerseys like a badge of honor and act as if we played a role in their performance. What happens when they are not doing well? Some abandon, others stay and hope for the next season. There is an emotional connection to the team and with all the other fans as we form a bond by association. Authors, we await their next book and rush out to get it. Why? We anticipate that it will meet our expectations and want it to as we feel connected to them through their writing. We are not wearing their jersey and high fiving each other with each chapter and yelling at the book to perform better but yet we feel connected to the author and other readers. As we start to think about the tools whether traditional advertising or social media that we can utilize to create brand loyalty we need to examine how we can create the loyalty by utilizing the tools.

## Six Ways to Create Brand Loyalty

**1. Be Better than Anyone.**
What is your one thing and how can you do it better than anyone? This is not to say to only have one product but more to focus on what you really do better than anyone else. Being better than anyone else does not allow for consumers to consider alternatives as they know that they cannot receive what they get with you elsewhere. **Chris Brogan** says it best in his **Do One Thing Very Well** post.

**2. Belonging.**

Create a sense of belonging whether it be via a "community" that is exclusive to your brand to give people a reason to want to wear that badge. Answer why should they be associated with you and loyal to you. Go beyond that we have a great product and identify why people would want everyone to know that they are connected to you.

### 3. Credibility.

This is more than doing what you say you will or a product that does what you say it will. Remember we are talking about how to build loyalty with the tools available. You may have a great product, message but your marketing materials are photo copied or a profile that is a template and not reflective of your brand identity. Well done, aesthetically pleasing and user focused organized websites, materials and profiles give a sense of credibility which leads to trust.

### 4. Accessibility.

This ties into belonging as if the "right" person is accessible, people want to be a part of to say that they "know" this person or the CEO of the company reached out to me. This is where the humanization of the brand comes in as we are able to connect and really let people know that behind the brand is a consumer, family man/woman, etc. who eats lunch, drinks coffee, etc.

**5. Connection ability.**

How do you speak to your audience? Learn to talk like they do or teach them how you want them to talk about you. This is widely used with tag lines and the brand message however there are times that a brand takes on a new "language" that is driven by the audience. Know this and adopt it (so long as it is what your brand represents). Outside Nevada, it is pronounced Na-vah-da where locally it is Neh-vada. While some may use the outside version locally to grab attention, the focus goes off of the product/service and becomes about how the name is not pronounced properly.

**6. Repeat.**

Stay on top of what consumers are saying and avoid being stale or changing too fast. Brands have a very long shelf life and those that are on top of where change or the shifts in the mindset of consumers are able to adapt and maintain loyal customers. Be proactive and not reactive to try and pull people back as once they are gone, they are gone.

Brand loyalty is more than the product itself. Yes, it has to perform well, actually better than any alternative so there is no alternative in the mind of the consumer but place this more in the aspect of behavior. Socially how does your product fit into their social development and why should it? Why should they want to be a part of your brand and what emotionally will they gain? In some areas it will be the perceived value vs. the quality (think laundry detergent) where with a television shows it is about the connection to the characters and the plot.

## BRAND POSITIONING

Brand positioning refers to "target consumer's" reason to buy your brand in preference to others. It is ensures that all brand activity has a common aim; is guided, directed and delivered by the brand's benefits/reasons to buy; and it focuses at all points of contact with the consumer.

Brand positioning must make sure that:

- Is it unique/distinctive vs. competitors?
- Is it significant and encouraging to the niche market?
- Is it appropriate to all major geographic markets and businesses?
- Is the proposition validated with unique, appropriate and original products?

- Is it sustainable - can it be delivered constantly across all points of contact with the consumer?

- Is it helpful for organization to achieve its financial goals?

- Is it able to support and boost up the organization?

In order to create a distinctive place in the market, a niche market has to be carefully chosen and a differential advantage must be created in their mind. Brand positioning is a medium through which an organization can portray it's customers what it wants to achieve for them and what it wants to mean to them. Brand positioning forms customer's views and opinions.

Brand Positioning can be defined as an activity of creating a brand offer in such a manner that it occupies a distinctive place and value in the target customer's mind. For instance-Kotak Mahindra positions itself in the customer's mind as one entity- "Kotak "- which can provide customized and one-stop solution for all their financial service's needs. It has an unaided top of mind recall. It intends to stay with the proposition of "Think Investments, Think Kotak". The positioning you choose for your brand will be influenced by the competitive stance you want to adopt.

Brand Positioning involves identifying and determining points of similarity and difference to ascertain the right brand identity and to create a proper brand image. Brand Positioning is the key of marketing strategy. A strong brand positioning directs marketing strategy by explaining the brand details, the uniqueness of brand and it's similarity with the competitive brands, as well as the reasons for buying and using that specific brand. Positioning is the base for developing and increasing the required knowledge and perceptions of the customers. It is the single feature that sets your service apart from your competitors. For instance- Kingfisher stands for youth and excitement. It represents brand in full flight.

There are various positioning errors, such as-

1. Under positioning- This is a scenario in which the customer's have a blurred and unclear idea of the brand.

2. Over positioning- This is a scenario in which the customers have too limited a awareness of the brand.

3. Confused positioning- This is a scenario in which the customers have a confused opinion of the brand.

4. Double Positioning- This is a scenario in which customers do not accept the claims of a brand.

Brand Positioning is how a product is perceived in the mind of consumer in relation to competitor's brand in the market. Positioning is act of placing a company's brand in consumer's minds over and against competitors in terms of characteristics and benefits that the brand does and does not offer.

- Attribute or Benefit
- Quality and Price
- Use or User
- Competition

According to Phillip Kotler, "Positioning is the act of designing the company's offering and image to occupy a distinctive place in the target market's mind."

"Positioning starts with the product, But Positioning is not what you do to the product. Positioning is what you do to the mind of the prospect."

Firms can position on the basis of:
- Attributes attached with product or services
- High-tech image of company
- Benefits
- Category of user using this product
- Comparison with competitors
- Entire range of services

If a **brand** is a collection of perceptions in the mind of the consumer, then **brand** positioning is "creating, maintaining and developing a unique perception (or specialty) about a brand in the mind of the consumer." In the modern world (where supply and choice far outweighs demand) positioning is the crux of the branding process. Successful (or unsuccessful) positioning can make (or break) a brand. For example, **Mercedes** stands for "luxury and class", while **BMW** stands for "power and performance" reflected in their slogan "the ultimate driving machine." **Coca Cola** is positioned as "the real cola" or the "classic cola" while **Pepsi** positioned itself as a cola for "the generation next" to create differentiation with Coke. While **7 Up**, which was a late entrant to the market, and couldn't really compete with the other two, positioned itself as the "un cola" providing an alternative to people who don't like cola.

In each of the above cases, the brands "own" a specialty they have carefully chosen for themselves, through heavy advertising and other awareness campaigns. The three most critical elements for successful positioning are:

1. The specialty should be different/unique
2. It should be credible.
3. It should be relevant/important

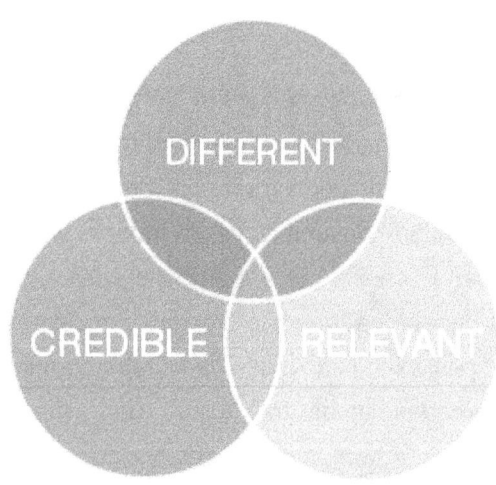

In each of the above examples, the specialties the brands own are unique, credible and relevant. FedEx changed the logistics services industry in US because it promised "overnight delivery" (a very important decision making criteria for their customers) and successfully fulfilled their promise every time ("when it absolutely, positively, has to be there overnight").

You will find lot of ways to determine successful brand positioning in various books including lot of matrices and graphs and charts. But here is a simple and very effective way to do it.

**Step 1:** Identify the key specialties in the industry you are operating in.
**Step2:** Narrow down the specialties into those that are unique, credible and relevant.
**Step 3:** Identify which others companies in your industry own these specialties.
**Step 4:** If there is any specialty left, you own it. If not, then you create a new sub category in your industry and become the number one in that sub category.
**Step 5:** Once you have decided a specialty for yourself, go hammer and tongs, promoting your specialty and associating your brand to it, by every possible means. Don't lose your focus and try to target other specialties.

It is far better to won a lesser important specialty (resulting in smaller audience size) no one owns, than to focus on a very important specialty, which is owned by a strong competitor. And your product may have many benefits, but stick to only the attribute you have chosen for yourself, to communicate in your advertising. No one remembers more than one idea. If you say too much, you say nothing, you are just making noise.

**BASICS OF BRAND POSITIONING**

Positioning is something (perception) that happens in the minds of the target market.

It is the aggregate perception the market has of a particular company, product or service in relation to their perceptions of the competitors in the same category.

It will happen whether or not a company's management is proactive, reactive or passive about the on-going process of evolving a position.

But a company can positively influence the perceptions through enlightened strategic actions.

In marketing, positioning has come to mean the process by which marketers try to create an image or identity in the minds of their target market for its product, brand, or organization. It is the 'relative competitive comparison' their product occupies in a given market as perceived by the target market.

Re-positioning involves changing the identity of a product, relative to the identity of competing products, in the collective minds of the target market.

De-positioning involves attempting to change the identity of competing products, relative to the identity of your own product, in the collective minds of the target market.

## THE PROCESS OF BRAND POSITIONING

Generally, the product positioning process involves:

- Defining the market in which the product or brand will compete (who the relevant buyers are)

- Identifying the attributes (also called dimensions) that define the product 'space'

- Collecting information from a sample of customers about their perceptions of each product on the relevant attributes

- Determine each product's share of mind
- Determine each product's current location in the product space
- Determine the target market's preferred combination of attributes (referred to as an ideal vector)
- Examine the fit between:

1. The position of your product

2. The position of the ideal vector

- Position.

The process is similar for positioning your company's services.

Services, however, don't have the physical attributes of products - that is, we can't feel them or touch them or show nice product pictures.

So you need to ask first your customers and then yourself, what value do clients get from my services? How are they better off from doing business with me? Also ask: is there a characteristic that makes my services different?

Write out the value customers derive and the attributes your services offer to create the first draft of your positioning.

Test it on people who don't really know what you do or what you sell, watch their facial expressions and listen for their response.

**ELEMENTS OF BRAND POSITIONING**

The **brand position** or **brand positioning** is how the brand is perceived in the context of competitive alternatives. As brand consultants, when we **develop brand positioning statements** for clients, we include a target customer definition, brand essence, brand promise, brand archetype and brand personality, giving the INTENDED brand position/positioning (as opposed to the actual brand position in the mind of the customer) greater depth.

The **unique value proposition** and **brand promise** are similar. They both focus on the one or two key points of difference between the brand in question and other brands. Typically, these points of difference are brand benefits, benefits that are relevant, unique, compelling and believable for the brand in question. Brands typically focus on only one or two benefits and research has shown that people can't link more than that number of benefits to a given brand in their minds. The first or most important benefit is sometimes referred to as the primary brand benefit. The unique value proposition for Volvo is "safety." As a brand promise, it could be expressed as "Only Volvo assures a safe ride to parents who care about their children's safety."

**Brand essence** is the "heart and soul" of the brand, its timeless quality, expressed as "adjective, adjective, noun." Some people refer to the brand essence as the brand mantra, while for others, the brand's mantra is synonymous with the brand's tagline or slogan.

Disney's brand essence: Fun family entertainment

Nike's brand essence: Authentic athletic performance

Starbuck's brand essence: Rewarding everyday moments

One usually talks about **attributes** associated with products. Generally, with brands, people focus on **benefits** or **values**. Brand benefits can be functional, emotional, experiential or self-expressive. Through market research, one can identify the path from attributes to benefits to values to self-esteem in customers' minds. This process is called **laddering**. A self-expressive benefit of the Mercedes brand is that it communicates that I have status and money.

**Brand associations** are anything that people link or associate with the brand in their minds. For example, people associate gambling and other vices with the Las Vegas, Nevada brand.

A **brand personality** is the composite of different brand personality elements. We focus on 7 to 12 brand personality elements for each brand. A **brand personality element** is usually expressed as an adjective. The purpose of brand personality attributes is to help personify the brand and to give it a distinctive "brand voice. Brand personality elements include the following: trustworthy, innovative, reliable, friendly, rugged, wholesome, etc. We explore 57+ common personality attributes with our clients.

A **brand archetype** is the underlying archetype that implies the driving force or motivation behind the brand. With the brand personality, the brand archetype gives a brand a more human feel. Brand archetypes include the pioneer, the wizard, the scientist, the sage and the artist. We explore 22+ common archetypes with our clients.

**Brand trigger** is a term used mostly in Europe. It refers to anything that is associated with the brand that causes people to think about the brand. It elicits brand recall. Some people refer to a brand trigger as a **brand mnemonic device**. So, most **brand identity elements** (name, tagline, logo, jingle, etc.) are or can be brand triggers. The GEICO gecko is a trigger for the GEICO brand.

In the **brand positioning** process it's important to understand your target market is ever-changing. You must continue to evaluate the market and your target customers -- those that are most important to the future of your brand. With this understanding, continue to re-visit your positioning and tighten the focus.

## BRAND POSITIONING STRATEGIES

A product can be positioned based on 2 main platforms: The Consumer and The Competitor. When the positioning is on the basis of CONSUMER, the campaigns and messages are always targeted to the consumer himself (the user of the product)

Peter England always campaigns their product concentrating on the consumer, the user of its product.

Louis Philip also concentrates on this kind of campaigns.

The other kind of positioning is on basis of competition. These campaigns are targeted towards competing with other players in the market.

Dettol television commercials always concentrate on advertisements, which show that this product would give you more protection, then the others.

A number of positioning strategies might be employed in developing a promotional program. The 7 such strategies are discussed below:

## POSITIONING BY PRODUCT ATTRIBUTES AND BENEFITS

Associating a product with an attribute, a product feature or a consumer feature. Sometimes a product can be positioned in terms of two or more attributes simultaneously. The price/ quality attribute dimension is commonly used for positioning the products.

A common approach is setting the brand apart from competitors on the basis of the specific characteristics or benefits offered. Sometimes a product may be positioned on more than one product benefit. Marketers attempt to identify salient attributes (those that are important to consumers and are the basis for making a purchase decision)

- Consider the example of Ariel that offers a specific benefit of cleaning even the dirtiest of

clothes because of the micro cleaning system in the product.
- Colgate offers benefits of preventing cavity and fresh breath.
- Promise, Balsara's toothpaste, could break Colgate's stronghold by being the first to claim that it contained clove, which differentiated it from the leader.
- Nirma offered the benefit of low price over Hindustan Lever's Surf to become a success.
- Maruti Suzuki offers benefits of maximum fuel efficiency and safety over its competitors. This strategy helped it to get 60% of the Indian automobile market.

**POSITIONING BY PRICE/ QUALITY**

Marketers often use price/ quality characteristics to position their brands. One way they do it is with ads that reflect the image of a high-quality brand where cost, while not irrelevant, is considered secondary to the quality benefits derived from using the brand. Premium brands positioned at the high end of the market use this approach to positioning. Another way to use price/ quality characteristics for positioning is to focus on the quality or value offered by the brand at a very competitive price. Although price is an important consideration, the product quality must be comparable to, or even better than, competing brands for the positioning strategy to be effective.

PARLE BISLERI – "BADA BISLERI, SAME PRICE" AD CAMPAIGN.

## POSITIONING BY USE OR APPLICATION

Another way is to communicate a specific image or position for a brand is to associate it with a specific use or application.

Surf Excel is positioned as stain remover 'Surf Excel hena!'

Also, Clinic All Clear – "Dare to wear Black".

## POSITIONING BY PRODUCT CLASS

Often the competition for a particular product comes from outside the product class. For example, airlines know that while they compete with other airlines, trains and buses are also viable alternatives. Manufacturers of music CD's must compete with the cassettes industry. The product is positioned against others that, while not exactly the same, provide the same class of benefits.

## POSITIONING BY PRODUCT USER

Positioning a product by associating it with a particular user or group of users is yet another approach.

Motography Motorola Mobile Ad. and this ad the persona of the user of the product is been positioned.

## POSITIONING BY COMPETITOR

Competitors may be as important to positioning strategy as a firm's own product or services. In today's market, an effective positioning strategy for a product or brand may focus on specific competitors. This approach is similar to positioning by product class, although in this case the competition is within the same product category.

Onida was positioned against the giants in the television industry through this strategy, ONIDA colour TV was launched with the message that all others were clones and only Onida was the leader. "Neighbor's Envy, Owners Pride".

## POSITIONING BY CULTURAL SYMBOLS

An additional positioning strategy where in the cultural symbols are used to differentiate the brands. Examples would be Humara Bajaj, Tata Tea, Ronald McDonald. Each of these symbols has successfully differentiated the product it represents from competitors.

www.ingramcontent.com/pod-product-compliance
Lightning Source LLC
Chambersburg PA
CBHW072031230526
45466CB00020B/1704